The Family Finance Fix
Strategies for Every Household Stage

Andrew Galowey

Copyright © [Andrew Galowey] [2024]. All rights reserved. No part of this publication may be reproduced, distributed, or transmitted in any form or by any means, including photocopying, recording, or other electronic or mechanical methods, without the prior written permission of the publisher, except in the case of brief quotations embodied in critical reviews and certain other noncommercial uses permitted by copyright law.

Table Of Contents

Introduction

Chapter 1: Laying the Foundation: Budgeting and Debt Management

Chapter 2: Growing Together: Planning for Young Families

Chapter 3: Building Your Nest, Financing Your First Home

Chapter 4: Weathering the Storm: Strategies for Midlife Families

Chapter 5: Reaping the Rewards: Secure Your Retirement

Conclusion

Introduction

You've started a wonderful journey: creating a family. However, along with the excitement, concerns emerge, such as how we might successfully manage our cash. How can we prepare for the future, regardless of what life throws at us?

The Family Finance Fix is your entire guide to attaining financial health throughout your family's existence. From the early days of budgeting as a newlywed pair to negotiating the complexity of retirement savings, this book offers practical solutions and guidance.

We'll simplify down financial jargon, answer your pressing concerns, and walk you through important subjects like budgeting, debt management, large spending planning, and wealth creation as a group.

Whether you're just starting out or well on your way, this book will help you make smart financial choices, accomplish your objectives, and provide a secure future for your loved ones.

Let us go on this financial adventure together to make your family's aspirations come true.

Chapter 1: Laying the Foundation: Budgeting and Debt Management

Congratulations! Have you recently married or intend to marry soon? Are you looking forward to a journey of love, laughter, and financial stability? Yes, finance. It may not be the most romantic subject, but a strong financial foundation is essential for a happy and secure future together. This chapter will provide you with the skills you need to lay that foundation, including a practical budget and a defined debt-reduction plan.

Budgeting: The Road Map to Financial Harmony

Consider a budget to be a road map for your family's money. It allows you to monitor your income and spending, guaranteeing that you do not spend more than you make. It also helps you prioritize your spending and meet your financial objectives, like as saving for a honeymoon, creating an emergency fund, or budgeting for the future.

Here's how to make your first budget together:

- Gather Your Information: The first step is to be transparent. Gather all of your income statements, including wages, side hustles, rental income, and so on. Next, list all of your costs, including rent/mortgage, utilities, food, transportation, entertainment, and any current debt payments. Be open and honest about everything, from regular coffee trips to monthly memberships.

- Choose a Budgeting Method: There are several budgeting strategies available; select one that works for you. Popular budgeting strategies include the 50/30/20 rule (50% necessities, 30% desires, 20% savings/debt repayment) and the zero-based budget (every dollar has a function).

- Monitor Your Spending: Awareness is essential. Track your monthly income and spending using a budgeting tool, a spreadsheet, or a basic pen and paper. This will uncover spending tendencies you may not have seen previously.

- Align Your objectives: Now comes the fun part: creating objectives! Is this a fantasy vacation? A down payment on a house? Discuss your short- and long-term objectives and include them in your budget.

- Talk and compromise: Budgeting is a team endeavor. Talk about your spending patterns and priorities freely. Be willing to sacrifice; you may have to change your regular coffee run or that new streaming service to free up finances for something more vital.

Mastering the Debt Monster

Many couples start marriage with some kind of debt, such as college loans, vehicle payments, or credit card liabilities. Don't allow debt put a strain on your relationship. Here are proven techniques for addressing it:

- List and categorize: Make a comprehensive list of all of your debts, including the amount outstanding, interest rate, and minimum payment. To prioritize payments, categorize them according to interest rate (highest to lowest).

Consider combining your high-interest debt. Look for a lower interest rate loan to consolidate your current bills into a more manageable monthly payment.

- Debt payback Strategies: Select a debt payback approach that complements your personality and objectives. Some possibilities include the avalanche approach (paying off debts with the highest interest rate first) and the snowball method (paying off lesser debts fast to boost motivation).

- Avoid New Debt: While paying off current debt, avoid incurring new debt. Consider alternatives, such as saving for major expenditures or using a rewards credit card that is paid off in full each month.

- Celebrate Your Milestones: Debt repayment is a marathon, not a sprint. Celebrate every accomplishment, whether it's paying off a credit card or a large portion of a debt. This will keep you motivated on your journey to financial independence.

Communication is key

Remember that finances are a team effort. Be upfront and honest with one another about your income, spending patterns, and financial concerns. Set up frequent check-ins to review your progress, revise the budget as required, and celebrate your successes together.

Building a sound financial foundation is a continuous effort. This chapter introduces the first tools and tactics. Your budget will grow and change with your family. However, with open communication, teamwork, and a dedication to your financial objectives, you'll be well on your way to a prosperous and secure future together.

Chapter 2: Growing Together: Planning for Young Families

Building a family gives enormous pleasure, but it also introduces new financial responsibilities. This chapter will help you understand the financial demands of young families with small children.

Cost of Tiny Humans

Let's face it: small ones are pricey! Diapers and formula, as well as daycare and clothing, may rapidly become expensive. Here's how to prepare for these expenses:

Childcare is often the largest expenditure for young families. Consider choices such as daycare facilities, nanny services, and in-home care. Investigate expenses in your location and include them into your budget.

- Health Insurance: Make sure your children have health insurance. Examine several plans and copays to choose the best match for your requirements.

- Children's rapid growth often leads to excessive eating. Consider increasing food prices for healthful meals and snacks.

- Clothing: Children grow out of garments quickly! Consider purchasing used clothing, using hand-me-downs, or creating a capsule wardrobe of mix-and-match items.

Budgeting for Growing Families

With a new member (or members!), it's time to review your budget. Here are a few tips:

- Track New costs: For one month, track all of your extra baby-related costs to obtain an accurate picture.

- Re-evaluate Needs vs. Wants: Change your budget to emphasize essentials. You may need to reduce some spending, such as entertainment or eating out, to cover the higher costs of having children.

- Embrace Frugal Fun: Being frugal does not imply abandoning fun. Explore free or low-cost activities such as visiting parks, libraries, or hosting movie nights at home.

Saving for the Future: Education and Beyond

The sooner you begin saving for your child's education, the better. Here are a few choices:

- 529 programs: These education savings programs provide tax benefits for college or vocational school.

- Coverdell Education Savings Accounts (ESAs): These accounts enable for tax-free donations towards eligible educational costs such as private school tuition or tutoring.

Creating an Emergency Fund

Unexpected costs are unavoidable, particularly with small children. Aim to accumulate an emergency fund that will cover 3-6 months of living expenditures. This will give a financial safety net in the event of a job loss, medical emergency, or vehicle maintenance.

Life Insurance Considerations

Life insurance offers financial security for your loved ones in the event of your death. Consider term life insurance, which provides reasonable coverage for a limited time.

The Power of Two Incomes

Many young families choose to have one parent remain at home with their children. If this is your goal, talk about the financial ramifications first. Can you live on one salary or will you need to supplement it? Consider choices such as freelance employment, internet enterprises, or part-time jobs.

Growing Together Financially

Raising a family is a team effort, and economics are no exception. Here are a few tips:

- Open Communication: Talk about your financial objectives and problems honestly.

- Establish common financial objectives, such as saving for a dream trip or a down payment on a home.

- Shared Responsibility: Take turns handling your money, whether it's budgeting, paying bills, or keeping track of costs.

Building a solid financial foundation for your young family requires preparation, communication, and collaboration. By using these tactics, you will be able to confidently negotiate the financial realities of early motherhood and provide a secure future for your children.

Chapter 3: Building Your Nest, Financing Your First Home

Homeownership! It's a fantasy for many couples, providing security, space, and a feeling of achievement. But navigating the world of mortgages and down payments may be intimidating. This chapter will provide you with the information and resources you need to successfully finance your first house.

The Mortgage Maze

Before you dive in, understand the many kinds of mortgages available.

Conventional loans need a minimum down payment of 3%. They are provided by private lenders and are not government insured.
- FHA Loans: Backed by the Federal Housing Administration, these loans require a reduced down payment (as little as 3.5%). However, FHA loans

need upfront and annual mortgage insurance costs.

- VA Loans: For qualified veterans and current military people, VA loans provide $0 down payment choices and reasonable interest rates.

Qualification for a Mortgage

Lenders evaluate your capacity to repay the loan based on a number of factors:

- Credit Score: A high credit score (preferably over 670) leads to reduced interest rates and better lending conditions.

- The Debt-to-Income Ratio (DTI) compares your monthly debt payments to your gross monthly income. A lower DTI (preferably less than 36%) increases your chances of qualifying for a mortgage.

- Employment History: A steady job with a regular salary reveals your capacity to make mortgage payments.

A greater down payment decreases the loan amount you need to borrow and your monthly payment.

The Power of Saving

Saving for a down payment is critical. Here are a few tips:

- Set a Savings Goal: Determine a reasonable down payment amount based on your budget and desired property price.

- Automate Savings: Set up automatic payments from your checking account to your savings account to gradually increase your down payment.

- Reduce Expenses: Look for areas in your budget where you may save money for your down payment. Consider making temporary concessions, such as dining out less or canceling subscriptions.

- Investigate Down Payment aid Programs: Many federal and municipal programs provide down payment aid to first-time homeowners. Discover what's available in your region.

Beyond the down payment

Remember, the down payment is not the only expense connected with homeownership. Consider closing charges, which may vary from 2 to 5% of the purchase price. These include costs for origination, appraisal, title insurance, and other services.

Budgeting for Home Ownership

Aside from your mortgage payment, there are extra continuing expenditures associated with property ownership. Be careful to consider in

- Property taxes: Your local government levies yearly taxes depending on the value of your house.

Homeowners insurance protects your property in the event of damage or tragedy. upkeep and Repairs: Owning a property requires periodic repairs as well as continuous upkeep bills.

House Hunting with Your Head (And Heart)

While location, size, and amenities are all essential, consider cost first. Do not get emotionally connected to a residence that exceeds your budget.

Working with a Realtor

A skilled realtor can help you navigate the home-buying process, negotiate offers, and advocate for your needs. Find an experienced and licensed realtor who specializes in first-time homebuyers.

The Journey to Homeownership

Purchasing your first house is a big milestone. You may approach the mortgage process with confidence if you prepare ahead of time, save money, and understand the steps. Remember that homeownership is a long-term commitment. Make sure you are financially prepared for the continuing expenses and duties. With careful planning and collaboration, your ideal house may become a reality.

Chapter 4: Weathering the Storm: Strategies for Midlife Families

Midlife presents a distinct set of financial concerns. Children may be leaving for college, occupations may be changing, and the golden years begin to take shape. This chapter will provide you with ideas for navigating the financial realities of midlife families.

The Balancing Act: Career Transitions and Earning Potential

Many midlife individuals change careers or reach a plateau in earning capacity. Here are several strategies to deal with these situations:

- Upskilling and Reskilling: To remain current in your industry, pursue continuing education, certifications, or online courses.

- Exploring New Opportunities: If your present work is no longer fulfilling you, consider changing paths. Look into prospective new vocations and their earnings potential.

- Side Hustles and the Gig Economy: Look for freelance jobs, internet enterprises, or part-time opportunities to augment your income.

Plan for College Costs

College may be a major financial strain. Here are some pressure-relieving strategies:

- College Savings Plans: If you haven't already, begin saving for college now. Use 529 plans or Coverdell ESAs to take advantage of tax breaks.

- Scholarships and Grants: Look into scholarships and grants that your kid may be eligible for to help pay for college.

- Financial assistance: Look into federal and state financial assistance possibilities to help with education expenditures.

The Sandwich Generation Squeeze

Many middle-aged individuals find themselves caring for both their elderly parents and their children. Here are some strategies to deal with this financial squeeze:

- Open Communication: Discuss money with your parents and children. Investigate possibilities for eldercare and college finance combined.

- Help your parents prepare for their anticipated long-term care requirements. Consider choices such as assisted living facilities and long-term care insurance.

- Government Assistance Programs: Look into government programs that may give financial assistance to your elderly parents.

Maximize Your Earning Potential

Here are some techniques to optimize your income potential in midlife.

- Negotiate Your Salary: Don't be hesitant to ask for a raise or promotion if you feel you deserve it. Look at the industry-standard salary for your job.

- Multiple Income Streams: Look into extra income opportunities outside of your principal work. Consider investing in rental properties, starting a side company, or doing consulting.

- Invest Wisely: Investing may help you accumulate money over time. Research several investing alternatives depending on your risk tolerance and financial objectives.

Debt Management Strategies

Midlife might be an ideal moment to address residual debt, such as college debts or mortgages. Here are a few strategies:

- Consolidating high-interest debt into a lower-interest loan may help you save money.

- Accelerated Repayment: Increase your monthly payments to pay off debt quicker and avoid interest costs.

- Balance Transfer Credit Cards: Use balance transfer credit cards with 0% introductory APR periods to strategically pay off debt (be aware of exorbitant fees after the promotional period).

Planning for Retirement

Retirement may feel far off, but midlife is the ideal time to increase your retirement resources. Here are a few tips:

- Increase Retirement Contributions: Increase your contributions to retirement accounts such as IRAs and employer-sponsored 401(k). Take advantage of any employer-matched contributions.

- Catch-Up Contributions: The IRS permits people over 50 to contribute more money to their retirement accounts each year.

- Review Your Retirement Plan: Review your retirement plan on a regular basis and alter your asset allocation to reflect your age and risk tolerance.

Weathering the Storm Together

Midlife may be a financially difficult period, but with open communication, smart preparation, and a dedication to your objectives, you can weather the storm. Remember, you are not alone. Discuss your financial issues with your spouse, and include your children in age-appropriate financial conversations. Working as a team allows you to negotiate the financial realities of midlife and provide a secure future for your family.

Chapter 5: Reaping the Rewards: Secure Your Retirement

Congratulations! You've achieved (or are about to reach) retirement age, which means you may relax, travel, and pursue your interests. However, a comfortable and joyful retirement is not an accident. This chapter will walk you through ideas for increasing your retirement funds and preparing for a comfortable and joyful senior years.

Creating Your Retirement Nest Egg

By now, you should have a good basis for retirement funds. Let's look at strategies to maximize it:

- Examine Your Retirement Accounts: Evaluate your present retirement funds in IRAs, 401(k), and other retirement plans. Consider your risk tolerance and time horizon before adjusting your asset allocation if necessary.

- Catch-Up Contributions: Do not underestimate the value of catch-up contributions. Every year, the IRS enables persons over the age of 50 to contribute more money to their retirement accounts. Take advantage of this chance to increase your nest egg.

- Maximize Employer Matching: Many businesses will match a percentage of your retirement contribution. Contribute enough to obtain the full employer match, which is practically free money!

- Explore Additional Savings Strategies: To supplement your retirement income, consider downsizing your house, investing in rental properties, or establishing a side gig.

Navigating Social Security Benefits

Social Security is an important source of income for many seniors. Here's what you should know.

- Claiming Age: You may claim Social Security payments as early as age 62, but your monthly income will be decreased. To maximize your benefits, you must wait until your full retirement age (FRA), which ranges from 66 to 67 years old depending on your birth year.

- Maximizing Benefits: Delaying collecting your benefits permits them to increase, resulting in a larger monthly payment during your retirement.

- Spousal Benefits: If you have been married for at least ten years, you may be eligible for spousal benefits based on your spouse's Social Security earnings record.

Plan for Healthcare Costs

Healthcare bills may be a considerable burden during retirement. Here are several methods to prepare:

- Medicare is a government health insurance program that is accessible to the majority of Americans at the age of 65. However, Medicare does not cover all medical expenses. To address coverage gaps, consider supplementary Medicare Advantage plans or Medigap policies.

- Contribute to an HSA if you have a high-deductible health plan. HSAs enable you to make pre-tax contributions to meet eligible medical costs.

- Long-Term Care Insurance: If you need assisted living or nursing care, consider purchasing long-term care insurance to help pay the expenses.

Creating a Retirement Budget

While your income is likely to reduce in retirement, your costs may not. Create a realistic retirement budget based on your expected income and desired lifestyle. Consider basic costs such as housing, utilities, healthcare, and food. Don't forget to budget for leisure activities, vacation, and hobbies.

Living within your means

Living within your means is key to a comfortable retirement. Avoid lifestyle inflation - do not allow your spending habits rise just because you are no longer working.

Review and adjust your plan

Retirement is a marathon, not a sprint. Your financial demands and circumstances will change over time. Review your retirement plan on a regular basis and make any necessary adjustments to your withdrawal method or budget.

Beyond the Nest Egg: Creating a Fulfilling Retirement

Retirement encompasses more than simply cash. Here's how to build a satisfying golden age:

- Pursue Your Passions: Retirement is an excellent time to try new hobbies, volunteer for issues you care about, or travel the globe.

- Stay Socially Connected: Social isolation may be difficult for retirees. Maintain positive connections with family and friends, and seek out ways to engage with your community.

- Stay Active: Physical and mental exercise are essential for sustaining your health and well-being throughout retirement.

Reap the rewards together

Retirement is a chapter full with opportunities. You may make your dream of a comfortable and joyful retirement a reality by planning ahead of time, optimizing your retirement resources, and budgeting for unforeseen needs. Remember, you do not have to go through this path alone. Discuss your retirement goals with your spouse, engage your children in age-appropriate financial conversations, and seek expert counsel if necessary. With careful preparation and open communication, you may enjoy the benefits of your efforts and create a bright future together.

Conclusion

You've completed our detailed guide on family finances. Consider this book a compass that will guide you through your family's financial journey. We've discussed budgeting techniques for newlyweds, the difficulties of preparing for young children, and the complications of financing your first house. We've also dealt with the realities of midlife money, such as employment shifts, college savings, and eldercare preparation. Finally, we've arrived at the golden years, providing you all the information you need to have a happy and joyful retirement.

Remember that financial well-being is an ongoing journey, not a one-time destination. As your family grows and changes, so will your financial requirements and objectives. Encourage open conversation with your husband and children; financial literacy is a family affair! Discuss your shifting circumstances, review your intentions, and commemorate your accomplishments along the road.

With the tools and techniques offered here, and driven by your steadfast dedication to your family's financial future, you may leave a legacy of stability and security for future generations. So, move on with your loved ones and achieve your financial objectives one step at a time. Remember that a secure financial future is more than simply numbers; it is about peace of mind, shared aspirations, and the ability to live a life filled with love, laughter, and lasting memories together.

www.ingramcontent.com/pod-product-compliance
Lightning Source LLC
Chambersburg PA
CBHW050250230526
45470CB00005B/2201